OXFORD SPELLING

Dr Tessa Daffern

STUDENT
BOOK

5

Name:

Class:

OXFORD
UNIVERSITY PRESS
AUSTRALIA & NEW ZEALAND

Oxford University Press is a department of the University of Oxford.
It furthers the University's objective of excellence in research,
scholarship, and education by publishing worldwide. Oxford is a registered
trademark of Oxford University Press in the UK and in certain other
countries.

Published in Australia by
Oxford University Press
Level 8, 737 Bourke Street, Docklands, Victoria 3008, Australia.

First published 2021

Reprinted 2023 (twice), 2024

ISBN 9780190326135

Reproduction and communication for educational purposes
The Australian *Copyright Act 1968* (the Act) allows educational institutions that
are covered by remuneration arrangements with Copyright Agency to reproduce
and communicate certain material for educational purposes. For more information,
see copyright.com.au.

Edited by Barbara Delissen
Cover illustration by Lisa Hunt
Illustrated by Lisa Hunt
Typeset by Integra Software Services Pvt. Ltd., Pondicherry, India
Proofread by Anita Mullick
Printed in China by Golden Cup Printing Co Ltd

Oxford University Press Australia & New Zealand is committed to sourcing
paper responsibly.

MIX
Paper | Supporting
responsible forestry
FSC
www.fsc.org   FSC™ C110497

Acknowledgements
The author and the publisher wish to thank the following copyright holders for reproduction of their material.

From *Fox* by Margaret Wild and illustrated by Ron Brooks. Text © 2004 Margaret Wild. Reproduced by permission
of Allen & Unwin p. 17; *Loyal Creatures* by Morris Gleitzman. Text copyright © Morris Gleitzman. First published
by Viking AU, 2014. Reprinted by permission of Penguin Random House Australia Pty Ltd, p. 13; *Harry Potter and
the Philosopher's Stone*: Copyright © J. K. Rowling, 1997, pp. 40, 51, 72; Shutterstock, pp. 19, 21, 28, 38, 55, 68, 74,
79, 93, 101; From *The Great Bear* by Libby Gleeson and illustrated by Armin Greder. Text © 1995 Libby Gleeson.
Reproduced by permission of Walker Books Australia, p. 24.

The 'Bringing it together' activities provided online are adapted with permission from Daffern, T. (2018). *The
components of spelling: Instruction and assessment for the linguistic inquirer.* Literacy Education Solutions Pty Limited.

Every effort has been made to trace the original source of copyright material contained in this book. The
publisher will be pleased to hear from copyright holders to rectify any errors or omissions.

WELCOME TO OXFORD SPELLING

Welcome to *Oxford Spelling Student Book 5*! This book contains 28 units that you will use across the year, and that will help you gain new spelling knowledge and skills.

You will notice that each unit is divided into three sections:

- **Phonology (green section)**
- Orthography (blue section)
- **Morphology (purple section).**

This has been done to guide you in the types of thinking you might use to answer the questions in each section.

Tip

- In the phonology sections, think about the sounds you can hear in words.
- In the orthography sections, think about the letter patterns that you know.
- In the morphology sections, think about the meaning of base words, prefixes and suffixes.

At the end of each unit, your teacher will work with you on a 'Bringing it together' activity. This is a chance to bring together all the things you are learning about spelling and apply them to new words!

Your teacher, along with the *Oxford Spelling* superheroes, will be giving you lots of helpful information as you work through this book. Look out for the tips in each unit for handy hints on how to answer questions.

Enjoy *Oxford Spelling*, and meet the two superheroes who will help you become super spellers – Stretchy Sienna and X-Ray Xavi!

A phoneme is the smallest speech sound you can hear in a word. For example, the word 'draw' has three phonemes: **/d/**, **/r/** and **/aw/**.

1 Count the syllables in each word. Sort the words using the table. Then count how many phonemes are in each word.

| scorched | enormous | morphological | tournament | laundry |

| automatic | haunt | pausing | Singaporean | enforceable |

Each syllable must have a vowel phoneme.

	Word	Number of phonemes
One-syllable words		
Two-syllable words		
Three-syllable words		
Four-syllable words		
Five-syllable words		

1 There are many ways to spell the **/aw/** phoneme (as in 'fork'). Find the letter patterns involving the **/aw/** phoneme in the words. Sort the words using the table. Then underline the letter pattern that involves the **/aw/** phoneme in each word.

astronaut   award   gourmet   audience   install   soar   carnivore

moor   jigsaw   cardboard   stall   reward   sought   ignore

sprawling   morphology   scorch   floor

walnut   withdraw   Singapore   thought

pause   source   absorb   towards

wharf   court   door   also

or	
aw	
ore	
al or *all*	
au	
our	
ar	
oor	
oar	
ough	

OXFORD UNIVERSITY PRESS

Homophones are words that sound the same but look different and have a different meaning.

'Write' and 'right' are homophones.

1 Complete each sentence with the correct homophone. You may use a dictionary to help you.

soar/sore/saw	draw/drawer	more/moor

poor/pour	source/sauce	raw/roar

a I _____ in my free time.

b The opposite of rich is _____.

c I love the taste of raspberry _____ drizzled over my fruit salad.

d Through our binoculars, we _____ a pod of whales.

e The yacht will _____ alongside the dock.

f Cook the chicken, because you will become sick if you eat it

_____.

g The cost of petrol is expected to _____ in the coming weeks.

h Please _____ a cup of tea.

i The smoke has made my eyes _____.

j I found a secret _____ in the desk.

k I would like to eat _____ of that tasty garden salad.

l One example of a renewable energy _____ is the sun.

m We could hear the _____ of the lions.

2 Write your own sentences using these homophones.

Word	Sentence
saw	
sore	
soar	
source	
sauce	
raw	
roar	

Now try this unit's 'Bringing it together' activity, which your teacher will give you.

UNIT 2

Tip

A disyllabic word is a word with two syllables. 'Science', 'complete' and 'breakfast' are all disyllabic words.

1. Say each word and clap along with the syllables. Notice that each word is disyllabic. In some of the words, the first syllable is the accented syllable (which means that syllable has the strongest emphasis). In other words, the second syllable is accented.

Sort the words using the table.

regain   dinner   annoy   undone   banner   knuckle

connect   moment   gentle   align   campaign

knowledge   design   knotted   maintain

Accented first syllable	Accented second syllable

2. Look for some more disyllabic words in a book you are reading. Add them to the table above.

6

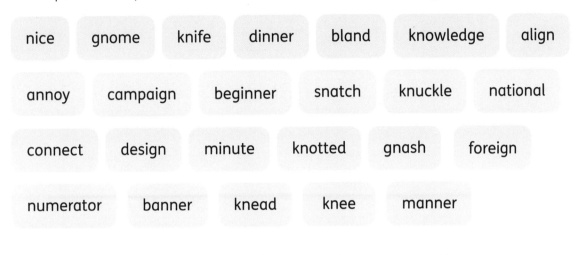

1. There are a few ways to spell the **/n/** phoneme (as in 'no'). Find the letter patterns that spell the **/n/** phoneme in the words. Sort the words using the table.

| nice | gnome | knife | dinner | bland | knowledge | align |

| annoy | campaign | beginner | snatch | knuckle | national |

| connect | design | minute | knotted | gnash | foreign |

| numerator | banner | knead | knee | manner |

n

nn

gn

kn

2. Write these words in alphabetical order in the table on the next page. Then write a definition for each word. You may use a dictionary to help you.

Then underline the letters that represent the **/n/** phoneme in each word.

| campaign | align | foreign | knead | gnash | numerator | cannon |

OXFORD UNIVERSITY PRESS

Word	Definition

Morphology

1 Complete each sentence with the correct homophone.

not/knot   need/knead   new/knew

a   Sofia _____ only plays guitar but she sings, too.

b   Bakers often use a machine to _____ large quantities of dough.

c   The sailor will _____ the rope before departing.

d   The painter will _____ blue and yellow paint to make green paint.

e   Luca decided to buy a _____ pair of shoes.

f   By using a recipe, the chef _____ how to bake the cake.

Now try this unit's 'Bringing it together' activity, which your teacher will give you.

OXFORD UNIVERSITY PRESS

UNIT 3

> **Tip**
>
> A schwa is an **/uh/** sound in a word. It can be heard in an unaccented syllable, and is not long or short. For example, the letter **a** in 'balloon' represents a schwa.

1 Say each word. Listen for the vowel sounds. Circle the words with a schwa.

invade	fraction	living	offspring	citizen
rotate	axis	television	graphs	region	dance
celebrate	morpheme	translate	action	phoneme
dimension	animal	technique	problem

> **Tip**
>
> A digraph is two letters that represent one phoneme, for example, **ch** and **oo**.
> A blend is speech sounds that join together in a word, for example, **/fr/** and **/str/**.

2 Choose four words from the last activity to complete the table. Underline any consonant digraphs you can find in the words. Circle any consonant blends. Then count the phonemes in each word.

Number of syllables	Word	Number of phonemes
One syllable		
Two syllables		
Three syllables		
Four syllables		

1 There are many ways to spell the **long /a/** phoneme (as in 'play'). Find the letter patterns that spell the **long /a/** phoneme in the words. Sort the words using the table. Use a dictionary to check the meaning of any words you don't recognise.

display   bait   rate   sleigh   paper   sundae   they   fiancée

steak   vein   reindeer   payment   cable   weight   investigate

attain   whey   break   betray   translate   matinée   obey

surveillance   detail   freight   native   vertebrae   veil

great   flavour   activate   eightieth   frail   fray

ay

ai

a-e

eigh

a

ae

ey

ea

ei

ée

OXFORD UNIVERSITY PRESS

> **Tip**
> Etymology is the study of where words come from and how they change over time.

1 Use an online etymology dictionary to find out the origin (place and time) of the words in the table. Write a definition for each word

Word	Origin	Definition
café		
purée		
gourmet		
beige		
mayonnaise		

> **Tip**
> A base word is the smallest part of a word that is also a word on its own. 'Sing' is a base word.
> A suffix is a letter or letters that go at the end of a word to make a new word. For example, **-s** is a suffix that can be added to the base word 'sing' to make a new word: 'sings'.

2 Use the rules and example words to complete the **present** tense sentences below and on the next page. Remember to add the suffix **-s** or **-es**.

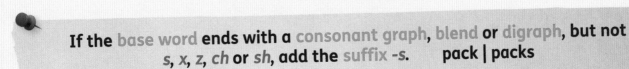

If the base word **ends with a** consonant graph, blend **or** digraph, **but not** s, x, z, ch **or** sh, **add the** suffix -s.   **pack | packs**

The grocer _____ vegetables into a box.

> **Tip**
> A graph is one letter representing one speech sound. For example, **b** in the word 'boy' represents the **/b/** sound on its own.
> A trigraph is three letters that represent one sound. For example, the letter pattern **tch** in 'catch' represents one sound: **/ch/**.

> **If the base word ends with s, x, z, ch or sh, or a consonant trigraph such as tch, add the suffix -es.   fix | fixes**

A mechanic _____ motor vehicles.

> **If the base word ends in a consonant and then y, change the y to i and add the suffix -es.   cry | cries**

My baby brother _____ when he is hungry.

> **If the base word ends in e, just add the suffix -s.   nibble | nibbles**

A fish _____ the bait.

A verb is a word for something that happens. 'Collect', 'investigate' and 'think' are all verbs.

3 Scan a book you are reading to find some base words that use the rules from the last activity. These words will be verbs. Write each base verb and then add the suffix **-s** or **-es**.

Rule	Example	Base verb	Verb with suffix **-s** or **-es**
1	pack | packs		
2	fix | fixes		
3	cry | cries		
4	nibble | nibbles		

Now try this unit's 'Bringing it together' activity, which your teacher will give you.

OXFORD UNIVERSITY PRESS

UNIT 4

Loyal Creatures
by Morris Gleitzman

While I fumbled for the money, Joan looked at me
sympathetically and Mrs Prescott looked at me like I was
something you find wriggling at the bottom of a bore hole.

But I knew all that could change.

If I came back from the war with a chest full of medals
all that could change, permanently.

1 Read the text above. Find words in the text to complete the table here and
on the next page.

A four-syllable word	
A five-syllable word	
Two words with three phonemes	
Two words starting with a consonant digraph	
Two words with four phonemes	
A two-syllable word with an unaccented final syllable	
A word with five phonemes	
Two words with six phonemes	
A word that rhymes with 'grind'	
A word that rhymes with 'stood'	

Two words that rhyme with 'store'	
A word that ends with a consonant blend	
A word that ends with a consonant digraph	
Two words with a medial long vowel phoneme	
Two words with a **short /e/** vowel phoneme	
Two words with a schwa in the final syllable	

1 Write these words in alphabetical order. Then write a sentence using each word.

receipt   ceiling   relief   complete   compete

reason   chimpanzee   beacon   guarantee

Word   Sentence

2 There are many ways to spell the **long /e/** phoneme (as in 'see'). Find the letter patterns that spell the **long /e/** phoneme in the words. Sort the words using the table.

breed	beacon	metre	concrete	brief	receipt	achieve	relief

equal	beneath	complete	receive	protein	extreme	ceiling

disagree	believe	eager	fever	theme	guarantee	genius	reason

ee	
ea	
ei	
e	
ie	
e-e	

1 Use the rules about the suffix **-ing** and the base words provided to complete the sentences below and on the next page, using each example word.

> **If the base word ends with a short vowel graph then a consonant graph, double the last letter and add the suffix -ing.**   clap | clapping

step	The dancers are _____ rhythmically across the stage.

> **If the base word ends with x, or with a consonant blend, digraph or trigraph, just add the suffix -ing.**   wash | washing

pack	We finished the board game, so now we're _____ up.

> **If the base word has a vowel digraph in the last syllable, just add the suffix -ing.**
> beep | beeping

| aim | The hikers are _____ to reach the mountain peak by midday. |

> **If the base word ends in y, or a vowel digraph or trigraph such as ow or igh, just add the suffix -ing.** sigh | sighing

| sow | Horticulturists are _____ seeds to grow vegetables. |

> **If the base word ends in e, usually drop the e and then add the suffix -ing.** smile | smiling

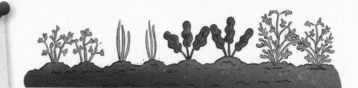

| gaze | My friends and I will be _____ at the stars tonight. |

2 Scan a book you are reading to find some base verbs that use the rules from the last activity. Write each base verb and then add the suffix **-ing**.

Rule	Example	Base verb	Verb with suffix **-ing**
1	clap | clapping		
2	wash | washing		
3	beep | beeping		
4	sigh | sighing		
5	smile | smiling		

Now try this unit's 'Bringing it together' activity, which your teacher will give you.

OXFORD UNIVERSITY PRESS

UNIT 5

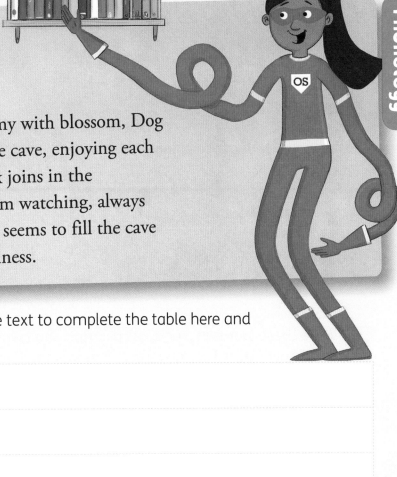

Fox
by Margaret Wild

In the evenings, when the air is creamy with blossom, Dog and Magpie relax at the mouth of the cave, enjoying each other's company. Now and again Fox joins in the conversation, but Magpie can feel him watching, always watching her. And at night his smell seems to fill the cave – a smell of rage and envy and loneliness.

1 Read the text above. Find words in the text to complete the table here and on the next page.

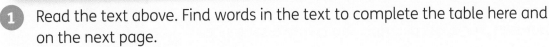

A two-syllable word	
All of the three-syllable words	
A four-syllable word	
Four words with three phonemes	
Four words with four phonemes	
Three words with five phonemes	
Three words with six phonemes	
A two-syllable word with an accented final syllable	
Three words starting with a consonant blend	
A word that rhymes with 'south'	
A word that rhymes with 'possum'	

A word that rhymes with 'stage'	
Four words that end with a consonant digraph	
Three words with a **long /a/** vowel phoneme	
Three words with a medial **long /e/** vowel phoneme	
A two-syllable word with a schwa	
A three-syllable word with a schwa	

1 Write these words in alphabetical order. Then write a sentence using each word. You may use a dictionary to help you.

quote	plateau	chateau	foe

dough	aloe	cockroach

Word	Sentence

OXFORD UNIVERSITY PRESS

2 There are many ways to spell the **long /o/** phoneme (as in 'boat'). Find the letter patterns that spell the **long /o/** phoneme in the words. Sort the words using the table.

cockroach   shallow   quote   echo   foe   dough   plateau

shown   locally   though   loaf   oppose   aloe   toe   moat

postage   elbow   episode   boast

bureau   program   woe   chateau

pillow   although   diagnose

oa	
ow	
o-e	
o	
oe	
ough	
eau	

OXFORD UNIVERSITY PRESS

1 Write sentences for each base word below. Use the rules to add different suffixes to each base word. The first one is done for you.

Tip

Think of these base words as verbs.
Don't forget to check the rules about suffixes from past units.
For rules about **-s** and **-es**, go to Unit 3, pages 11 and 12.
For rules about **-ing**, go to Unit 4, pages 15 and 16.

Base word	Suffix	Sentence
oppose	**-s** or **-es**	Kayla <u>opposes</u> my suggestion to leave.
	-ing	Kayla is <u>opposing</u> my suggestion to leave.
annoy	**-s** or **-es**	
	-ing	
receive	**-s** or **-es**	
	-ing	
knot	**-s** or **-es**	
	-ing	
quote	**-s** or **-es**	
	-ing	
scorch	**-s** or **-es**	
	-ing	
display	**-s** or **-es**	
	-ing	
connect	**-s** or **-es**	
	-ing	
break	**-s** or **-es**	
	-ing	

Now try this unit's 'Bringing it together' activity, which your teacher will give you.

UNIT 6

1 Say each word. Listen for the **long /oo/** phoneme. Use the words to complete the table.

lagoon	acoustics	tomb	truthfully
throughout	screw	pollutant	bamboo
improving	proof	monsoonal	

Three words with one syllable	
Three words with two syllables	
Three words with three syllables	
All words with three phonemes	
All words with four phonemes	
All words with five phonemes	
All two-syllable words with an accented final syllable	
Three words starting with a consonant blend	
All words rhyming with 'through'	
All words starting with a vowel	
Three words with a **long /oo/** phoneme in the second syllable	

1 There are many ways to spell the **long /oo/** phoneme (as in 'blue'). Find the letter patterns that spell the **long /oo/** phoneme in the words. Sort the words using the table.

blue	through	bruise	acoustics	pollute
screw	fluid	womb	accrue	absolute	lagoon
youth	truth	brew	fruit	tomb	bamboo
soup	knew	scoop	juice	remove	throughout
flute	cue

ue

oo

u-e

ew

ou

u

ui

o

ough

OXFORD UNIVERSITY PRESS

2 Write these words in alphabetical order. Then write a sentence using each word. You may use a dictionary to help you.

| lagoon | bruise | acoustics | accrue | womb | absolute |

Word	Sentence

Tip

Regular verbs are verbs that can have a suffix added to change tense. Regular verbs take the suffix **-ed** to make past tense. Sometimes the base verb needs to change when the suffix is added.

1 Use the rules about the suffix **-ed** to write sentences in past tense, using each example word.

If the base word **ends with a short** vowel graph **then a** consonant graph **other than x, double the last letter and then add the** suffix -ed.   **drag | dragged**

_____

If the base word **ends with x, or with a** consonant blend, digraph **or** trigraph, **just add the** suffix -ed.   **wash | washed**

_____

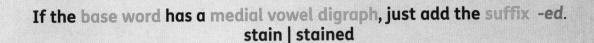

If the base word **has a** medial vowel digraph, **just add the** suffix *-ed*.
stain | stained

_____

If the base word **ends in a** vowel digraph **or** trigraph **such as** *ay,*
ow, er, **or** *igh,* **usually just add the** suffix *-ed*.   **spray | sprayed**

_____

If the base word **ends in** e, **drop the** e **then add the** suffix *-ed*.   **scramble | scrambled**

_____

If the base word **ends in a** consonant **and then** *y,*
change the *y* **to** *i,* **then add the** suffix *-ed*.   **tidy | tidied**

_____

2 The following text has some missing past tense verbs. Use the base words to help you write the missing past tense verbs. Use the rules from the last activity to check your spelling.

The Great Bear   by Libby Gleeson

To the music of trumpets, drums, and cymbals, she _____.
dance

She _____ her feet and _____ to the sound, and
lift   sway

some in the crowd _____ and _____. Others
clap   cheer

_____ her with sticks and threw stones at her ragged coat.
poke

Now try this unit's 'Bringing it together' activity, which your teacher will give you.

OXFORD UNIVERSITY PRESS

UNIT 7

1   Say each word. Listen for the **long /i/** phoneme. Use the words to complete the table.

| encyclopedia | enlighten | glide | environmental | haiku | kaleidoscope |

| feisty | capsize | classify | tie | slight | dehydration | biological |

One-syllable words	
Two-syllable words	
Three-syllable words	
Four-syllable words	
Five-syllable words	
Six-syllable word	
Words that start with the same two phonemes	
Words starting with a consonant blend	
Words with a **long /i/** phoneme in the second syllable	
Words that end with a vowel phoneme	
A word that rhymes with 'surprise'	
A word that rhymes with 'frighten'	

1 There are many ways to spell the **long /i/** phoneme (as in 'light'). Find the letter patterns that spell the **long /i/** phoneme in the words. Sort the words using the table below and on the next page.

Tip

Use a dictionary to check the meaning of any unfamiliar words.

| enlighten | pry | glide | pie | environmental | bonsai |

| behind | capsize | frightful | classify | tie | haiku |

| slight | Dubai | dehydrate | biology | define | die |

| Thailand | tonight | encyclopedia | describe | climate |

| kaleidoscope | Einstein | lie | feisty | unwind | knight |

| time | find | brightly | line | sighing | shy | fly |

igh

y

i-e

ie

OXFORD UNIVERSITY PRESS

i

ai

ei

2 Choose six words from the last activity. Write these words in alphabetical order. Then write a descriptive sentence for each of the words. You may use a dictionary to help you.

Word	Sentence

1 Complete each sentence with the correct homophone. You may use a dictionary to help you.

site/sight   time/thyme   bite/bight

a The gentle dog does not growl or _____.

b Several families visited the _____ of the new school.

c I planted parsley, basil and _____ in my garden.

d The _____ of the rainbow was delightful.

e After art class, it was _____ to go home.

f A curve in a coastline or river is called a

_____.

2 Write a sentence for each homophone.

Words	Sentences
site	
sight	
time	
thyme	
bite	
bight	

Now try this unit's 'Bringing it together' activity, which your teacher will give you.

OXFORD UNIVERSITY PRESS

An unvoiced phoneme is a speech sound made using your breath rather than your voice, such as **/sh/** in 'shop'.

A voiced phoneme is a speech sound made using your voice, such as **/zh/** in 'measure'.

1 Say each word. Listen for the unvoiced **/sh/** phoneme.
Use the words to complete the table.

| accomplishment | brochure | viciously | chef | socialising | gush |

| special | distinguishable | parachute | mention | machine | magician |

Two one-syllable words	
Two two-syllable words	
Two three-syllable words	
Two four-syllable words	
A five-syllable word	
Two words with **/sh/** as the third phoneme	
Two words with **/sh/** as the fourth phoneme	
Words starting with a consonant blend	
Words with a **/sh/** phoneme in the third syllable	
Words that start with the same two phonemes	
A word that rhymes with 'flush'	
A word that starts with a consonant digraph	

1 There are many ways to spell the unvoiced **/sh/** phoneme (as in 'shop'). Find the letter patterns that spell the unvoiced **/sh/** phoneme in the words. Sort the words using the chart.

accomplish   brochure   caution   vicious   mission   chef   social

patient   session   gush   passion   special   distinguish   parachute

mention   establish   machine   station   magician   pension

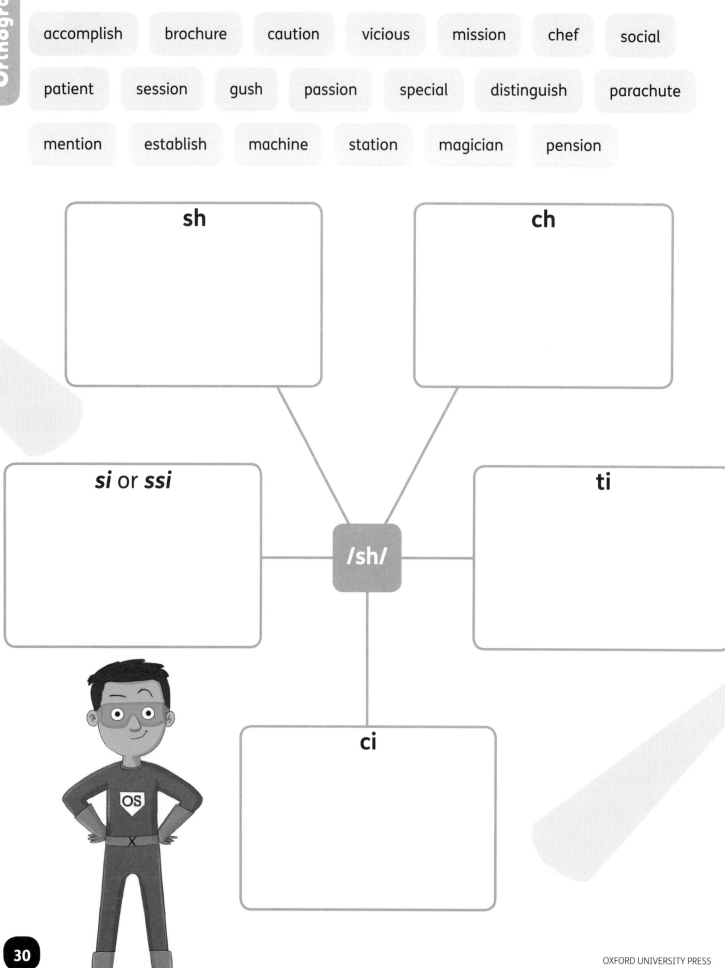

sh

ch

si or *ssi*

/sh/

ti

ci

OXFORD UNIVERSITY PRESS

Tip

The suffix **-ian** is used to form nouns describing a person. For example, a guardian is a person who guards or looks after something or someone.

1 Use the nouns with suffixes to complete the sentences.

dietician   musician   electrician   comedian   Olympian

mathematician   librarian   politician   historian

a Someone who studies mathematics is a _____.

b Someone who helps people maintain a healthy diet is a _____.

c Someone who works in politics is a _____.

d Someone who studies history is a _____.

e Someone who works with electricity is an _____.

f Someone who works in a library is a _____.

g Someone who performs comedy is a _____.

h Someone who competes at the Olympics is an _____.

i Someone who performs music is a _____.

Now try this unit's 'Bringing it together' activity, which your teacher will give you.

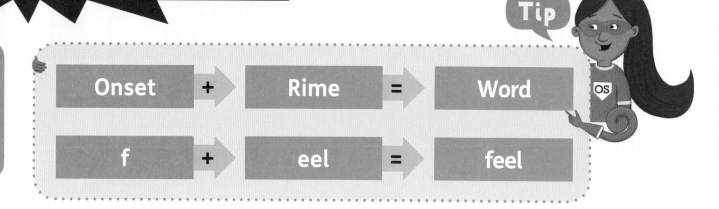

Tip

Onset	+	Rime	=	Word
f	+	eel	=	feel

1 Write words using these onsets and rimes.

Onsets	*f*, *b*, *d*, *c*, *g*, *l*, *m*, *n*, *kn*, *p*, *s*, *t*, *w*, *wh*, *y*, *z*, *ch*, *sh*, *st*, *dr*, *sm*, *gr*, *sp*, *sk*, *sch*, *squ*					
Rimes	*ell* as in 'fell'	*ill* as in 'fill'	*all* or *awl* as in 'fall' or 'bawl'	*ull* as in 'cull'	*ool* as in 'cool'	*eel* or *eal* as in 'steel' or 'steal'

Words that end with *ell*, as in 'fell'	Words that end with *ill*, as in 'fill'	Words that end with *all* or *awl*, as in 'fall' or 'bawl'	Words that end with *ull*, as in 'cull'	Words that end with *ool*, as in 'cool'	Words that end with *eel* or *eal*, as in 'steel' or 'steal'

1 There are many ways to spell the **/s/** phoneme (as in 'send'). Find the letter patterns involving the **/s/** phoneme in the words. Sort the words using the table.

script   assessment   false   balance   participate   scientific   castle

psyche   assortment   abundance   ascend   psychiatry

lapse   season   social   psychology   fossil   possum

decide   muscle   landscape   glisten   convince

psychotherapy   nestle   civic   discipline   audience

glimpse   reverse   bustle   acid

s

ss

se

ce

ci

sc

st

ps

Tip

The suffixes **-ance** and **-ence** derive from Latin. They can be added to the end of some words to make nouns that mean a quality or state. Sometimes they can also make words that describe an action or a process. For example, adding the suffix **-ance** to the word 'appear' makes a new word, 'appearance', which means how something appears.

1 Read these rules about the suffixes **-ance** and **-ence**.

> **If the base word is a verb that ends in *y*, change the *y* to *i* and add the suffix *-ance*.** defy | defiance

> **If the base word is a verb that ends in *ear*, add the suffix *-ance*.** appear | appearance

> **If the base word is a verb that ends in *ure*, remove the final *e* and add the suffix *-ance*.** insure | insurance

> **If the base word is an adjective that ends in *ant*, remove these three letters and add the suffix *-ance*.** brilliant | brilliance

> **If the base word is an adjective that ends in *ent*, remove these three letters and add the suffix *-ence*.** intelligent | intelligence

> **If the base word is a verb that ends in *ere*, remove the final *e* and add the suffix *-ence*.** interfere | interference

2 Use the rules to complete the table on the next page. Carefully consider the base words when deciding which rule to use. The first few are done for you.

OXFORD UNIVERSITY PRESS

Base word	Word with suffix (-*ance* or -*ence*)
defy	defiance
appear	appearance
insure	insurance
brilliant	brilliance
intelligent	intelligence
interfere	interference
excellent	
confident	
important	
significant	
vary	
assure	
cohere	
adhere	
elegant	
comply	
absent	
clear	

Now try this unit's 'Bringing it together' activity, which your teacher will give you.

1 Write words using these onsets and rimes.

Onsets	c, d, f, g, h, j, m, p, r, s, t, y, sh, cl, sm, fl, st, sc, gl		
Rimes	**ear**, **eer** or **ere** as in 'near', 'steer' or 'here'	**are**, **ear** or **air** as in 'dare', 'pear' or 'stair'	**ar** as in 'car'

Words that end with **ear**, **eer** or **ere**, as in 'near', 'steer' or 'here'	Words that end with **air**, **ear** or **air**, as in 'stair', 'pear' or 'dare'	Words that end with **ar**, as in 'car'

1. There are many ways to spell the **short /e/** phoneme (as in 'bed'). Find the letter patterns that spell the **short /e/** phoneme in the words. Sort the words using the chart below.

mellow   expression   pleasurable   jealousy   again   treasure

dimension   element   threatening   against   electricity

said   measure   temperature   develop   feather

dreading   investigate   leather

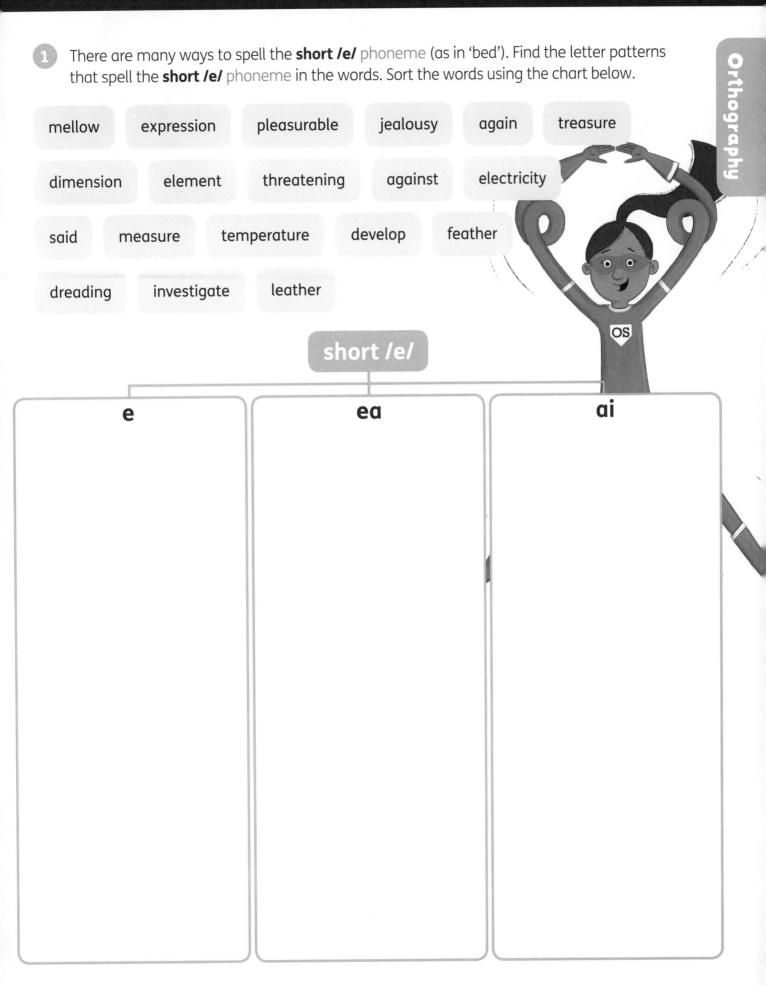

short /e/

e	ea	ai

2. Look in a book you are reading. Find some more words with a **short /e/** phoneme. Add them to the chart above.

3 Write these words in alphabetical order. Then write a definition for each word. You may use a dictionary to help you.

| mellow | expression | electricity |

| dimension | threatening | temperature |

Word	Definition

1 Use the base verbs in the tables to write sentences. Add the suffixes shown in each table to change the tense of your sentences. You may use a dictionary to check the meaning and spelling of any tricky words. The first one in each table is done for you.

Base verb	Sentence using base verb + suffix **-s** or **-es**
dance	The ballet student **dances**.
repeat	
carry	
compose	
access	
step	

OXFORD UNIVERSITY PRESS

Base verb	Sentence using base verb + suffix *-ed*
dance	The ballet student **danced**.
repeat	
carry	
compose	
access	
step	

Base verb	Sentence using base verb + suffix *-ing*
dance	The ballet student is **dancing**.
repeat	
carry	
compose	
access	
step	

Now try this unit's 'Bringing it together' activity, which your teacher will give you.

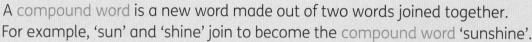

A compound word is a new word made out of two words joined together. For example, 'sun' and 'shine' join to become the compound word 'sunshine'.

Harry Potter and the Philosopher's Stone
by J. K. Rowling

Although owls normally hunt at night and are hardly ever seen in daylight, there have been hundreds of sightings of these birds flying in every direction since sunrise. Experts are unable to explain why the owls have suddenly changed their sleeping pattern.

1 Read the text above. Find words in the text to complete the table.

All two-syllable words starting with a consonant blend	
Two three-syllable words	
Two compound words	
Three words starting with a consonant digraph	
Three words with four phonemes	
A two-syllable word with an accented final syllable	
A two-syllable word with an unaccented final syllable	
Three words with six phonemes	

OXFORD UNIVERSITY PRESS

A word that rhymes with 'remain'	
A word with eight phonemes	
A word that rhymes with 'inserts'	
A word that starts with an **/ow/** diphthong	
Two words that start with a consonant blend and end with a consonant digraph	

1 There are many ways to spell the **/j/** phoneme (as in 'jug'). Find the letter patterns involving the **/j/** phoneme in the words. Sort the words using the table.

journal   lodge   region   cringe   adjective   suggestion   nudge

scrounge   adjustment   reject   adjudicate   hygiene   pyjamas

nostalgia   wedge   surgeon   exaggerate

j	
dge	
gg	
ge	
dj	
gi	

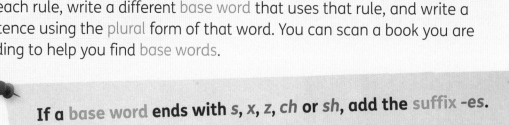

A plural noun is a word that tells us that there are two or more of something. 'Tigers' and 'dishes' are plural words.

The suffixes **-s** or **-es** can be added to many nouns to make plural words. 'Tigers' has the **-s** suffix. 'Dishes' has the **-es** suffix.

1 Use the rules to write the missing plural nouns in the sentences. Then, for each rule, write a different base word that uses that rule, and write a sentence using the plural form of that word. You can scan a book you are reading to help you find base words.

If a base word ends with s, x, z, ch or sh, add the suffix -es.

| coach | Our netball team has two _____. |
| | |

If a base word ends in f or fe, it is usual to change the f or fe to a v and then add the suffix -es.

| bookshelf | The bookstore has cats sleeping on the _____. |
| | |

If a base word ends in e, just add the suffix -s.

| castle | We visited two ancient _____. |
| | |

If a base word ends in a vowel and the letter o, add the suffix -s.

ratio	In maths class, we learned about percentages and _____ .

If a base word ends in a consonant and then o, it is usual to add the suffix -es.

potato	The farmer harvested a large crop of _____ .

If a base word ends in a consonant and then y, change the y to i and then add the suffix -es.

family	Our _____ came together to celebrate.

Now try this unit's 'Bringing it together' activity, which your teacher will give you.

OXFORD UNIVERSITY PRESS

1 Say each word. Listen for the voiced phonemes and unvoiced phonemes. Sort the words using the table.

performance   movement   rhythm   choreography

mouth   conservation   thousand   photography

voice   gather   weather   marathon

Words with a /f/ phoneme (unvoiced)	Words with a /v/ phoneme (voiced)

Words with an unvoiced /th/ phoneme	Words with a voiced /th/ phoneme

2 Now scan a book you are reading to find some more words to add to the table.

Tip

The letter **v** doesn't go by itself at the end of a word. If a word ends with the /v/ phoneme, it usually ends with the letters **ve**.

1 Complete the word search.

w	e	k	w	f	c	k	a	u	y	i	n	v	i	t	e	t	r	t	r
r	t	l	v	e	o	x	i	o	s	i	t	i	v	e	r	z	u	p	f
g	y	e	m	n	v	i	f	i	i	t	a	k	f	g	h	g	o	l	g
a	x	v	a	p	p	r	o	v	e	e	u	q	d	u	c	n	a	t	y
v	b	e	l	y	l	t	r	m	b	g	v	u	t	b	j	i	e	s	k
h	y	l	n	z	p	o	s	i	t	i	v	e	h	s	v	e	x	s	p
i	o	w	l	e	c	t	i	v	e	h	g	v	t	g	o	v	e	f	k
r	u	f	e	s	t	i	v	e	f	j	m	b	t	j	w	s	e	r	e
e	d	v	v	u	u	o	y	a	v	k	r	c	z	d	e	i	s	t	e
f	r	e	f	u	r	j	m	a	s	s	i	v	e	g	l	t	e	d	e
v	e	b	p	i	n	r	a	c	t	i	v	e	q	s	s	i	f	t	s
e	n	m	w	n	a	t	i	v	e	k	z	x	a	y	p	v	h	g	h
r	q	m	c	v	i	s	i	t	o	r	o	e	i	e	y	i	d	m	f
j	u	n	e	x	r	c	r	r	i	y	t	b	n	q	f	r	p	o	p
k	o	m	l	h	o	v	t	h	s	d	l	m	i	f	h	t	e	d	s

visitor
vowel
level
invite
active
positive
native
approve
festive
massive

A **/v/** phoneme is usually followed by a vowel. **Tip**

2 Read aloud from a book you are reading. See if you can find some words with the **/v/** phoneme. Write three of these words into the table, along with the sentences you found them in. Then, in each word you wrote in the left column, underline the letter **v** and the vowel that comes after it.

Word with **/v/** phoneme   Sentence

The suffix **-er** can be used to change a base verb to a person noun. For example, the verb 'teach' can be changed to the noun 'teacher', and the verb 'lead' can become the noun 'leader'.

Tip

1 Read the following rules and examples about using the **-er** suffix to make nouns that describe people. To each table, add base verbs that can become nouns using **-er.** Then change each base verb into a person noun, and use the noun in a sentence.

If the base word ends in e, drop the e and then add the suffix -er.

Verb	Person noun with **-er** suffix	Sentence
dance	dancer	The professional <u>dancer</u> performed in a ballet.

If the base word ends with a short vowel graph then a consonant graph, double the last letter and add the suffix -er.

Verb	Person noun with **-er** suffix	Sentence
swim	swimmer	The competitive <u>swimmer</u> won a gold medal at the Olympics.

Now try this unit's 'Bringing it together' activity, which your teacher will give you.

UNIT 13

> A diphthong is a kind of long vowel sound that you make by moving your mouth in two ways. For example, **/ow/** in the word 'cow' and **/oi/** in the word 'boy' are diphthongs.
>
> Also notice that your mouth changes shape when you say the **long /a/** phoneme, in words such as 'play'. This is also a diphthong.

1 Say each word. Listen for the diphthong. Sort the words using the table.

allow   enjoy   contain   poison   portray   flower   android

trousers   retain   betray   towel   ointment

Words with **/ow/** phoneme	Words with **/oi/** phoneme	Words with **long /a/** phoneme

2 Each of the words below has one of these diphthongs: **/ow/** (as in 'cow' and 'sound'), **/oi/** (as in 'boy' and 'coin') or **long /a/** (as in 'say' and 'rain').

Say each word and decide which words are correct. Circle each correct word and then write the correctly spelled word in the space provided. Underline the diphthong in each word that you have written. You may use a dictionary to check your answers.

a	fointain	fountain	faintain	_____
b	avoid	avaid	avowd	_____
c	disploy	displow	display	_____
d	empayer	empower	empoyer	_____
e	surround	surraind	surroind	_____
f	cloim	cloum	claim	_____
g	jount	jaint	joint	_____

1 Read the sentences. Some words have missing letters that represent the diphthong /ow/ (as in 'cow'). Choose either **ow** or **ou** to complete these words.

a   The colour of the wood is **br_____n**.

b   The bells in the **t_____er** ring at midday each day.

c   The **m_____ntain** is inhabited by goats.

d   The upset child is **fr_____ning**.

e   The wind was **p_____erful** during the storm.

f   I received a $10 **disc_____nt** when I bought a new comic book.

g   Mum and Dad are **pr_____d** of my efforts.

h   The large **cr_____d** was singing and dancing at the music festival.

i   Our Prime Minister made an important **ann_____ncement**.

j   The tea pot has a lovely curved **sp_____t**.

2 Read the sentences. Some words have missing letters that represent the diphthong /oi/ (as in 'boy'). Choose either **oy** or **oi** to complete the words.

a   Please do not **destr_____** the document.

b   I **av_____d** going outside on rainy days.

c   The dog's constant barking became **ann_____ing**.

d   There is a great deal of **m_____sture** in the rainforest.

e   The snake wrapped itself around in a **c_____l**.

f   We **enj_____** going to the cinemas with our friends.

g   The chef added pasta to the pot of **b_____ling** water.

h   Ming was being **l_____al** when he told the truth.

i   The ship arrived in Antarctica after a six-month **v_____age**.

j   Some plants are **p_____sonous**.

Tip

An adjective is a word that tells us what something is like.

The suffix **-er** can be added to some adjectives to compare things. For example, 'rougher' and 'smoother' are two adjectives that could be used to compare different textures.

As explained in Unit 12 (page 46), when the suffix **-er** is used with a verb, it can indicate a person noun. For example, 'diver' is a noun that describes a person. It comes from the base verb 'dive'.

1 Read each word. Notice that the words all end with the letters **er**. Sort the words using the table to show what the role of the word ending is. Use the examples to help you.

rougher   slower   dancer   larger   baker   shower   brighter

water   cheer   leader   hotter   surfer   greener   driver

suffer   drummer   safer   ladder   swimmer   answer   helicopter

The suffix **-er** forms an adjective that compares	The suffix **-er** forms a person noun	**er** is part of the base word
softer	painter	feather

2 Read the rules below and on the next page. Use the rules to add the suffix **-er** to each base word. Then write a sentence using each word with a suffix. The first one is done for you.

 If the base word ends in e, drop the e and then add the suffix -er.

Base word	Base word + **-er** suffix	Sentence
fine	finer	My baby sister's hair is <u>finer</u> than my hair.
brave		
late		

If the base word ends with a short vowel graph then a consonant graph, double the last letter and add the suffix -er.

Base word	Base word + -er suffix	Sentence
big	bigger	Microscopes make small things look <u>bigger</u>.
fit		
hot		

If the base word ends with a consonant and then y, change the y to i and add the suffix -er.

Base word	Base word + -er suffix	Sentence
dirty	dirtier	The streets have become <u>dirtier</u> in recent weeks.
easy		
heavy		

Now try this unit's 'Bringing it together' activity, which your teacher will give you.

OXFORD UNIVERSITY PRESS

Harry Potter and the Philosopher's Stone

by J. K. Rowling

He was tall, thin and very old, judging by the silver of his hair and beard, which were both long enough to tuck into his belt. He was wearing long robes, a purple cloak which swept the ground and high-heeled, buckled boots.

1 Read the text above. Find words in the text to complete the table.

A two-syllable word	
A two-syllable word with an accented final syllable	
A two-syllable word ending with a vowel phoneme	
A two-syllable word ending with a consonant digraph	
A word with six phonemes	
A word with a schwa in the final syllable	
A word starting with a consonant digraph	
A word starting with a consonant blend	
A word that rhymes with 'found'	
A word that rhymes with 'stepped'	
A word that rhymes with 'feared'	
A word with a **long /o/** phoneme	
A word with a **short /u/** phoneme	
A one-syllable word ending with an unvoiced phoneme	

1 There are many ways to spell the **/aw/** phoneme (as in 'fork'). The words below have the **/aw/** phoneme but some letters are missing. Choose from the letter patterns listed in the table to write the missing letters. Then write the words in the table.

Tip

Use a dictionary to check the spelling of these words if you are not sure.

n_____mal   _____thor   ch_____k   r_____ing   ign_____

t_____nament   br_____t   ind_____   rew_____d   f_____n

abs_____bing   dr_____ing   th_____t   l_____nch   sw_____m

w_____k   h_____d   g_____met   expl_____

or
aw
au
al
ar
oar
oor
ore
our
ough

> **Tip**
>
> The suffix **-est** can be added to the end of a base word to mean 'most'. This is called a superlative suffix. 'Highest' and 'brightest' are two words that use this superlative suffix.
>
> The green building is the **tallest** in the city.

 1 Use the rules below and on the next page to write sentences using words with suffixes.

If the base word ends in e, drop the e and then add the suffix -est.

Base word	Sentence
fine	The old coastal village is the <u>finest</u> in the state.
brave	
late	

 If the base word ends with a short vowel graph then a consonant graph, double the last letter and add the suffix -est.

Base word	Sentence
fit	Olympic athletes are the <u>fittest</u> people I know.
big	
hot	

If the base word ends with a consonant and then *y*, change the *y* to *i* and add the suffix -est.

Base word	Sentence
dirty	We washed the <u>dirtiest</u> clothes separately.
easy	
heavy	
tiny	
noisy	

Now try this unit's 'Bringing it together' activity, which your teacher will give you.

OXFORD UNIVERSITY PRESS

UNIT 15

> An r-influenced vowel is a vowel that sounds different because it is followed by the letter **r**. Examples are **/er/** in 'mermaid' and **/air/** in 'chair'.

1 These words have an r-influenced vowel phoneme. Sort the words using the table.

confirm   scarce   heartfelt   compared   harshest   nervously

rehearsal   shard   welfare   sergeant   carving   despair   aquarium

disturbance   circuit   yearn   repair

earnest   hilarious   startled   darkest

millionaire   archway   courtesy

Words with **/er/**, as in 'her'	Words with **/air/**, as in 'pear'	Words with **/ar/**, as in 'dark'

1 There are many ways to spell the **/er/** phoneme (as in 'her'). The words below have the **/er/** phoneme but the letters that spell this phoneme are missing. Choose from the letter patterns in the table to write the missing letters. Then write the words in the table.

Tip

Use a dictionary to check the spelling of these words if you are not sure.

conf_____m   adv_____b   reh_____sal   agricult_____

somb_____   w_____king   th_____sty   fig_____s

l_____n   dist_____b   des_____ve   j_____nal

w_____th   cent_____   occ_____   rig_____ous

ir	*er*	*ear*	*ur*
ure	*or*	*our*	*re*

Tip

Sometimes the **/er/** phoneme can sound a little different, depending on the way a person pronounces it. Sometimes it can sound like a schwa, an **/uh/** sound, but the spelling doesn't change.

OXFORD UNIVERSITY PRESS

Things That Are Most in the World
by Judi Barrett

The **silliest** thing in the world is a chicken in a frog costume.

The **hottest** thing in the world is a fire-breathing dragon eating a pepperoni pizza.

1 Write a creative sentence for each base word. Each sentence must use a comparative suffix (**-er**) and a superlative suffix (**-est**) added to the base word. Underline the words with suffixes in each sentence. Use the example to help you and the rules on pages 49–50 (**-er**) and pages 53-54 (**-est**).

Base word	Sentence using **-er** and **-est** suffixes
crazy	A laughing apple is <u>crazier</u> than a laughing dog but the <u>craziest</u> thing in the world is a laughing duck in a frog costume.
brave	
hot	
heavy	
smooth	
tasty	
fine	

Now try this unit's 'Bringing it together' activity, which your teacher will give you.

1 These words have an r-influenced vowel phoneme. Sort the words using the table.

| smearing | startled | beware | assert | assortment | garbage |

| chart | sheer | fair | disappear | convert | absorbed | ignore |

| circuit | repair | sincere | wharf | rehearse | atmosphere |

| stark | bollard | aerodynamic |

| firmly | prepare | formal |

Words with **/air/**, as in 'chair'	
Words with **/ar/**, as in 'start'	
Words with **/ear/**, as in 'near'	
Words with **/er/**, as in 'her'	
Words with **/aw/**, as in 'form'	

2 Now add some more words with **/air/**, **/ar/**, **/ear/**, **/er/** and **/aw/** phonemes to the table, using a book you are reading.

OXFORD UNIVERSITY PRESS

1 There are many ways to spell the **/k/** phoneme (as in 'kite'). The words below have the **/k/** phoneme but the letters that spell this phoneme are missing. Choose from the letter patterns in the table to complete the words. Then write the words in the table.

Tip

Use a dictionary to check the spelling of these words if you are not sure.

_____olour   _____oala   sti_____y   te_____nology   uni_____

sul_____   e_____idna   opa_____   s_____raps   _____ilometre

bu_____et   nap_____in   atta_____   psy_____ology   _____aos

artisti_____   magi_____al   bouti_____

c	k	ck	ch	que

Tip

The suffixes **-able** and **-ible** mean 'able to be'. They can be added to the end of some base words to form an adjective, such as 'enjoyable' and 'flexible'. The suffix **-able** is more common than the suffix **-ible**.

The suffix **-able** can generally be used when a complete word comes before it. But, for words ending in the phoneme **/s/**, it is common to use **-ible** instead. The suffix **-ible** is also commonly used after an incomplete word.

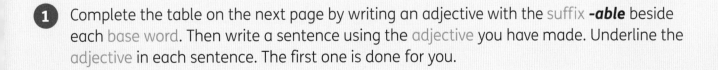

1 Complete the table on the next page by writing an adjective with the suffix **-able** beside each base word. Then write a sentence using the adjective you have made. Underline the adjective in each sentence. The first one is done for you.

Base word	Adjective with -able suffix	Sentence
manage	manageable	The task that we did in class was <u>manageable</u>.
adapt		
consider		
change		
reason		
knowledge		

2. The adjectives in the table end with the suffix **-ible**. Underline the suffix **-ible** in each word. Write the matching base verb. Then write a sentence using the adjective. Underline the adjective in each sentence. The first one is done for you.

If the base word ends in e, usually drop the e and then add the suffix -ible.

Adjective with -ible suffix	Base verb	Sentence
collaps<u>ible</u>	collapse	The <u>collapsible</u> table could easily fit in the tiny room.
convertible		
accessible		

OXFORD UNIVERSITY PRESS

3 Read the adjectives in the table. They end in the suffix **-ible** but the group of letters that comes before the suffix in each word does not make a complete word on its own.

Circle the suffix in each adjective and underline the part of the word that comes before the suffix. Then write a sentence using the adjective. The first one is done for you.

Adjective with -ible suffix	Sentence
leg(ible)	The handwritten letter is legible.
visible	
negligible	
impossible	

4 Use an online etymology dictionary to find out about the origin (time and place) of the words in the table. Write a definition for each word.

> **Tip**
> The **que** ending of these words spells the **/k/** phoneme.

Word	Origin	Definition
unique		
antique		
boutique		

Now try this unit's 'Bringing it together' activity, which your teacher will give you.

Tip

A consonant blend can occur in any part of a word. Examples are given below.

Initial position (at the start of a word)	Medial position (in the middle of a word)	Final position (at the end of a word)
/st/ in 'stop'	**/nd/** in 'landing'	**/mp/** in 'jump'

1 Say each disyllabic word. Listen for the consonant blend. Sort the words using the table. Then underline the consonant blend in each word you wrote.

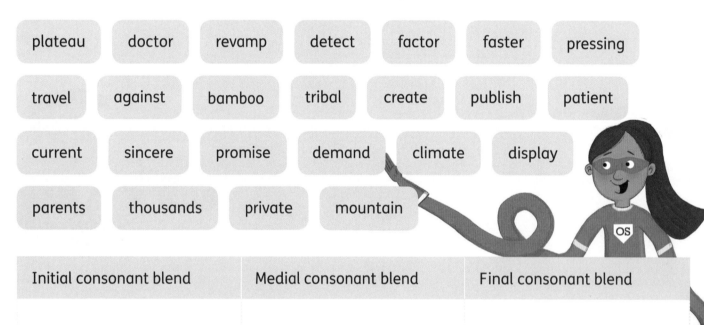

plateau	doctor	revamp	detect	factor	faster	pressing
travel	against	bamboo	tribal	create	publish	patient
current	sincere	promise	demand	climate	display
parents	thousands	private	mountain

Initial consonant blend	Medial consonant blend	Final consonant blend

1 There are many ways to spell the **long /a/** phoneme (as in 'play'). Some words in the sentences below have the **long /a/** phoneme but the letters that spell this phoneme are missing. Choose from these letter patterns to complete the words: **a**, **a-e**, **ae**, **ai**, **ay**, **ea**, **ée**, **ei**, **eigh** or **ey**. Then write the completed words in the table on the next page.

Tip

Use a dictionary to check the spelling of these words if you are not sure.

a   The items in the shop were on **displ_____**.

b   **V_____ns** transport blood through the body.

c   The spy **betr_____ed** his allies.

d   Please provide more **det_____l** in your report.

e   I **celebr____t____** the new year with my friends.

f   The train was hauling lots of heavy **fr_____t**.

g   The old man was thin and **fr_____l**.

h   **N____tive** plants attract beautiful birds to my backyard.

i   The fresh herbs added **fl____vour** to the soup.

j   We went to see the **matin_____** performance of the new musical.

k   The detectives **investig____t_____** the crime scene.

l   Snakes have lots of **vertebr____**.

m   We visited my grandmother for her _____**tieth** birthday.

n   We took our dogs to the beach and **th_____** enjoyed it very much.

o   I love to eat **st_____k** when it is cooked on the barbecue.

p   It is important to **ob_____** the road rules.

q   Be careful kicking the ball so you don't **br_____k** a window.

r   **R_____ndeer** can be found in the forests of Finland.

s   The man was very excited to marry his **fianc_____**.

ay

ai

a-e

eigh

a

ae

ey

ea

ei

ée

1 Complete each sentence with the correct homophone. You may use a dictionary to help you.

| maid/made | grate/great |

a The soccer match was _____.

b The _____ was asked to tidy the queen's bedroom.

c I _____ zucchini, cheese and carrots to make the pie.

d I _____ a pencil case out of wood.

Now try this unit's 'Bringing it together' activity, which your teacher will give you.

> **Tip**
>
> A consonant digraph can occur in any part of a word. Examples are given below.

Initial position (at the start of a word)	Medial position (in the middle of a word)	Final position (at the end of a word)
sh in 'shop'	**pp** in 'happy'	**ng** in 'bonding'

1 Say each disyllabic word. Look and listen for the consonant digraph. Sort the words using the table. Then underline the consonant digraph in each word you wrote.

| thousand | birthday | perish | princess | carry | Thursday |

| children | dancing | burrow | offer | photo | feather |

| banish | autumn | champion | dolphin | bucket | chimney |

| stomach | endless | fashion | thunder | beneath | shower |

Initial consonant digraph	Medial consonant digraph	Final consonant digraph

1 There are many ways to spell the **long /e/** phoneme (as in 'sleep'). The words below have the **long /e/** phoneme but the letters that spell this phoneme are missing. Choose from the letter patterns in the table to complete the words. Then write the words in the table.

Tip

Use a dictionary to check the spelling of these words if you are not sure.

br_____d   b_____con   m_____tre   concr_____t_____   br_____f

rec_____pt   ben_____th   chimpanz_____   compl_____t_____   ach_____ve

rec_____ve   bel_____ve   f_____ver   th_____m_____   disagr_____

_____ger   guarant_____   c_____ling   extr_____m_____   rel_____f

r_____son   g_____nius   _____qual

ee
ea
e
e-e
ie
ei

OXFORD UNIVERSITY PRESS

1 Add the suffix **-ate** to the base words in the tables below and on the next page. Then write each word with a suffix in a sentence. Use each rule and example to help you. You may use a dictionary to help you.

If the base word ends in e, it is usual to drop the e before adding the suffix -ate.

The suffix **-ate** can be added to some words to form an adjective meaning 'full of something'.

Base word	Base word + suffix **-ate**	Sentence
fortune	fortunate	I was <u>fortunate</u> to have won the prize.
affection		
passion		

The suffix **-ate** can also make a verb that describes a process.

Base word	Base word + suffix **-ate**	Sentence
captive	captivate	The singers <u>captivate</u> the audience.
active		
valid		

The suffix **-ate** sometimes forms a noun referring to a group of people or a place.

Base word	Base word + suffix **-ate**	Sentence
elector	electorate	More than half of the <u>electorate</u> voted.
consul		

2 Complete each sentence with the correct homophone. You may use a dictionary to help you.

cheap/cheep   read/reed

a   The baby birds will _____ when they are hungry.

b   The discounted vegetables were quite _____.

c   They picked a fresh green _____ from the riverbank.

d   Most of the news that I _____ is on the internet.

Now try this unit's 'Bringing it together' activity, which your teacher will give you.

UNIT 19

1 Say each word. Listen for the vowel phonemes in the middle and end of these words. Sort the words using the table.

| crooked | throughout | arrow | wooden | mistook | swallowing |

| parachute | mellow | absolute | hollow | footage | sooty |

| although | include | boutique | acoustics | doughnut | shouldn't |

Words with a **short /oo/** phoneme, as in 'book'	Words with a **long /o/** phoneme, as in 'grow'	Words with a **long /oo/** phoneme, as in 'grew'

2 Now scan a book you are reading to find more words that have these phonemes. Add the words to the table.

Tip

Remember that a diphthong is a kind of long vowel sound that you make by moving your mouth in two ways. Notice that the **long /o/** phoneme in words like 'boat' is a diphthong.

1 There are many ways to spell the **long /o/** phoneme (as in 'grow'). Some words in the sentences below have the **long /o/** phoneme but the letters that spell this phoneme are missing. Choose from the letter patterns in the table to complete the words. Then write the completed words in the table.

a The **cockr_____ch** scurried along the ground.

b The **m_____t** around the castle is full of crocodiles.

c A **f_____** is regarded as an enemy.

d The baker kneaded the **d_____** to bake loaves of bread.

e We watched a funny **epis____d____** on television last night.

f Tadpoles are swimming in the **shall_____** ponds.

g A **plat_____** can be described as a flat area on high ground.

h I grazed my **elb_____** when I fell off my bike.

i The doctor looked at the footballer's scan to **diagn____s____** the broken bone.

j The letter requires a **p_____stage** stamp so that it can be delivered.

k The **al_____** vera plant can grow in a sunny spot in the garden.

l I went to the **l_____cal** shops to buy milk and bread.

m A **chat_____** can be described as a fancy French castle or country house.

n It is cold, even **th_____** it is a sunny day.

oa
ow
o-e
o
oe
ough
eau

1 Complete each sentence with the correct homophone.
You may use a dictionary to help you.

sew/sow	rode/road	roe/row	tow/toe

a Fish eggs are called _____.

b The dressmaker will _____ a new dress.

c The truck will _____ the broken-down car to the mechanic.

d We _____ our bikes to the skate park.

e It is a lovely day to _____ the boat on the river.

f An accident caused traffic congestion on the _____.

g I stubbed my _____ on the edge of the step.

h The farmer will _____ the seeds in the field.

2 Write sentences using these homophones.

Words	Sentences
sew	
row	
tow	
rode	

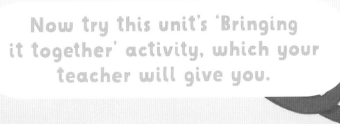

Now try this unit's 'Bringing it together' activity, which your teacher will give you.

Harry Potter and the Philosopher's Stone

by J. K. Rowling

He was almost twice as tall as a normal man and at least five times as wide. He looked simply too big to be allowed, and so *wild* – long tangles of bushy black hair and beard hid most of his face, he had hands the size of dustbin lids and his feet in their leather boots were like baby dolphins. In his vast, muscular arms he was holding a bundle of blankets.

1 Read the text above. Find words in the text to complete the table.

A two-syllable word	
A three-syllable word	
A two-syllable word with an accented final syllable	
Three two-syllable words that end in a vowel phoneme	
A compound word	
Two words with four phonemes	
A word with five phonemes	
A word with six phonemes	

OXFORD UNIVERSITY PRESS

Two words with seven phonemes	
Two words with a **/f/** phoneme (unvoiced)	
A word ending with a vowel digraph	
Two words ending with a consonant digraph	
Two words starting with a consonant blend	
Two words with a schwa in the final syllable	
A word with an **/ow/** diphthong	
A word with a **long /o/** phoneme	
A word that rhymes with 'vascular'	
A word that rhymes with 'feather'	

1 There are many ways to spell the **long /oo/** phoneme (as in 'moon'). Some words in the sentences on the next page have the **long /oo/** phoneme but the letters that spell this phoneme are missing. Choose from the letter patterns in the table following the sentences to complete the words. Then write the completed words in the table.

a   My favourite colour is **bl_____**.

b   The waiter added a spoon of sugar to the **br_____ed** tea.

c   We went paddling in the **lag_____n**.

d   Car emissions **poll ____t ____** the air.

e   **Bamb_____** is a fast-growing and versatile plant.

f   The carpenter will **scr_____** the cupboards to the wall.

g   Water is an example of a **fl ____ id**.

h   The pharaohs of ancient Egypt were buried in pyramid-shaped **t ____ mbs**.

i   We were **absol ____t ____ ly** sure it would rain.

j   I got a **br_____se** on my leg after bumping into the table.

k   The old man jumped out of bed with **y_____thful** vigour.

l   A baby grows inside a mother's **w____mb**.

m   It is better to tell the **tr____th** than to lie.

n   The train travelled **thr_____** a long, dark tunnel.

o   Our class can **accr_____** bonus points for assisting at the school fair.

p   The tropical **fr_____t** salad was a highlight of the meal.

q   The musicians were satisfied with the **ac_____stics** in the concert hall.

| *ue* |
| *oo* |
| *u-e* |
| *ew* |
| *ou* |

u

ui

o

ough

1 Complete each sentence with the correct homophone. You may use a dictionary to help you.

flew/flue/flu   root/route   lute/loot   cruise/crews

a Influenza is commonly known as the _____.

b A _____ is a musical instrument that looks similar to a guitar.

c Construction _____ worked together to build the skyscrapers.

d We used a map to find the quickest _____ to the beach.

e Excess smoke was rising up the chimney _____.

f Police captured the thieves carrying a bag of _____.

g Carrots, onions and turnips are _____ vegetables.

h It was so windy that my hat _____ through the air.

i The plane will _____ at an altitude of 40 000 feet.

Now try this unit's 'Bringing it together' activity, which your teacher will give you.

UNIT 21

1 Say each word. Listen for the **long /e/** phoneme or **long /i/** phoneme. Sort the words using the table.

| client | extreme | believe | silent | delight | region | feisty | cycle |

| satellite | species | receipt | height | sequence | scientist |

| divide | retrieve | antique | intrigue | subscribe | machine |

Long /e/ phoneme, as in 'see'	**Long /i/** phoneme, as in 'sight'

2 Now scan a book you are reading to find some more words that have these phonemes. Add the words to the table.

OXFORD UNIVERSITY PRESS

1 There are many ways to spell the **long /i/** phoneme (as in 'side'). Some words in the sentences below have the **long /i/** phoneme but the letters that represent this phoneme are missing. Choose from the letter patterns in the table below to complete the words. Then write the completed words in the table. You may use a dictionary to help you.

a   The damaged boat may **caps____z____** in the heavy seas.

b   The librarian will **classif____** the books by subject.

c   Addressing **env____ronmental** issues is a priority.

d   The information you provided is very **enl_____tening**.

e   I was shown how to bake an apricot **p_____**.

f   Play between the kittens became a little **f_____sty**.

g   A **bons_____** plant is a miniature tree.

h   The arrival of the train was **sl_____tly** delayed.

i   Drink plenty of water so you don't **deh____drate**.

j   The artist will **descr____b____** how the portrait was created.

k   The teacher often wears a vibrantly coloured **t_____**.

l   I enjoy the temperate **cl____mate** on the coast.

m   A **h_____ku** is a traditional form of Japanese poetry.

n   The light show was a **kal_____doscope** of colours.

igh	
y	
i-e	
ie	
i	
ai	
ei	

A morpheme is the smallest unit of meaning in a word.

Some words have more than one morpheme. For example, the word 'jumping' has two meaningful parts: the base word **jump** and the suffix **-ing**.

The morpheme **auto** means 'self'.

1 Add the morpheme **auto** to the start of the words below. Then write a definition. You may use a dictionary to help you. The first one is done for you.

Word	Definition
auto biography	A book someone has written about their own life
_____matic	
_____graph	

Tip

The morpheme **tele** means 'far'.

2 Add the morpheme **tele** to the start of the words below. Then write a definition. You may use a dictionary to help you. The first one is done for you.

Word	Definition
tele phone	A device that sends and receives sound over a distance
_____scope	
_____vision	

OXFORD UNIVERSITY PRESS

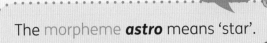

3 Add the morpheme **astro** to the start of the words below. Then write a definition. You may use a dictionary to help you. The first one is done for you.

Word	Definition
astro nomy	The science of stars and all aspects of the physical universe
_____naut	
_____metry	

Tip

The morpheme **bio** means 'life'.

4 Add the morpheme **bio** to the start of the words below. Then write a definition. You may use a dictionary to help you. The first one is done for you.

Word	Definition
bio logy	The scientific study of life
_____graphy	
_____diversity	

Now try this unit's 'Bringing it together' activity, which your teacher will give you.

Phonology

1 Say each disyllabic word. Notice that each word has an accented syllable and an unaccented syllable. Sort the words using the table.

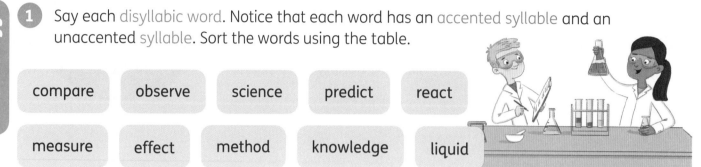

compare   observe   science   predict   react

measure   effect   method   knowledge   liquid

First syllable is accented	Second syllable is accented

2 Now find 10 more disyllabic words from a topic that you are studying in class at the moment. Add the words to the table.

Orthography

1 Say each word. Look at the letter patterns at the end of each word. Notice that each word ends with **le**, **al** or **el**. Underline the letter pattern at the end of each word.

bottle   tunnel   animal   local   travel   people   ankle

oval   channel   sprinkle   article   moral   chemical   towel

OXFORD UNIVERSITY PRESS

Tip

The letter pattern **le** can appear in the final position (at the end of a word). It is not usual, though, to see the final position letter pattern **le** after an **m**, **n**, **r**, **v** or **w**.

2 These base words end in **le**. Say each word. Sort the words using the tables.

| table | circle | sparkle | eagle | puzzle | shuffle | middle |

| people | bottle | drizzle | nibble | wrinkle | gentle | article |

| struggle | stifle | bristle | ripple | whistle | paddle |

Words ending in **ble**	Words ending in **cle**	Words ending in **kle**	Words ending in **dle**	Words ending in **gle**

Words ending in **fle**	Words ending in **ple**	Words ending in **tle**	Words ending in **stle**	Words ending in **zle**

Tip

Many adjectives can be changed to nouns by adding the suffix **-ness**. This suffix refers to a state of being.

Adjective	+	Suffix	=	Noun	Meaning of noun	Noun in a sentence
happy	+	**-ness**	=	happiness	The state of being happy	I wish you happiness.

Morphology

> **If the base** adjective **ends in** *y*, **usually change the** *y* **to** *i* **before adding the** suffix *-ness*.

1 Complete the table by writing sentences. In each sentence, include a noun made with each adjective and the suffix **-ness**. The first one is done for you.

Adjective	Sentence
drowsy	Because of my drowsiness, my eyes were growing heavy.
loud	
weak	
aware	
joyful	
thoughtful	
dark	
lazy	
fit	
empty	
fresh	

The following morphemes derive from Greek.

Greek morpheme	*hydro*	*eco*	*photo*
Meaning	water	home	light

Tip

OXFORD UNIVERSITY PRESS

2 Complete each word by adding a Greek morpheme. Then write a definition for each word. You may use a dictionary to help you. A few are done for you.

Word	Definition
<u>hydro</u>electricity	Electricity that is generated by moving water
_____plane	
<u>eco</u>system	A community or home where living things are linked together
_____logy	
<u>photo</u>graph	A picture made by using a sensor or plate that's sensitive to light
_____synthesis	

Now try this unit's 'Bringing it together' activity, which your teacher will give you.

1 Say each word. Listen to the initial consonant blend at the start of each word. Sort the words using the table.

shred   stranded   spreadable   sprawling   scrambling   shrinkable

screeching   scribbles   strangeness   shrieked   sprinkled   strategy

Words starting with **/shr/**	Words starting with **/scr/**	Words starting with **/str/**	Words starting with **/spr/**

2 Read each sentence and decide which consonant blend is needed at the start of the incomplete words. Choose from the letter patterns **shr**, **scr**, **str** or **spr** to complete the words. You may use a dictionary to help you.

a   The dog _____**atched** the door.

b   The jockey _____**addled** the horse.

c   Moving the heavy furniture was a _____**enuous** task.

d   Ferrets were _____**ounging** around in the blackberry bushes.

e   The athletes were _____**inting** to the finish line.

f   Heavy fog _____**ouded** the village.

g   The archer's arrow _____**ang** off the bow with great velocity.

h   I _____**ugged** my shoulders in despair.

1 Say each base word. Notice the letter patterns at the end of the final syllable of each word. Sort the words using the table.

| endeavour | eager | vinegar | alligator | tenor | foyer | flavour |

| grammar | sugar | scissor | monitor | neighbour | order | cover |

| nectar | pillar | alter | mirror | savour | rigour |

| Words ending in **or** | Words ending in **our** | Words ending in **er** | Words ending in **ar** |

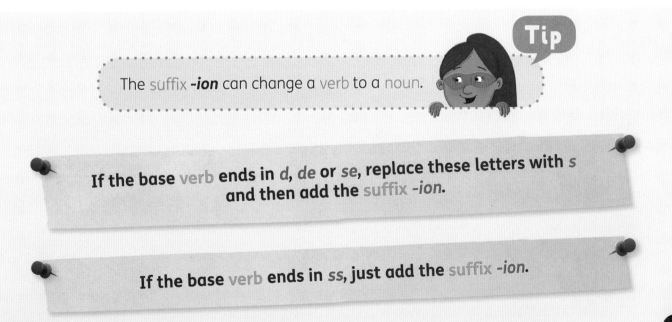

Tip

The suffix **-ion** can change a verb to a noun.

If the base verb ends in *d*, *de* or *se*, replace these letters with *s* and then add the suffix *-ion*.

If the base verb ends in *ss*, just add the suffix *-ion*.

1 Read each verb in the table. Change each verb to a noun by
adding the suffix *-ion*. Remember to use the rules on the
previous page to help you. You may use a dictionary to help you.

Base verb	Noun with -ion suffix	Use the noun with *-ion* suffix in a sentence
conclude	conclusion	The audience applauded at the <u>conclusion</u> of the performance.
erode		
divide		
explode		
decide		
discuss		
revise		
extend		

OXFORD UNIVERSITY PRESS

2 Write the base verb for each noun with a suffix. You may then use a dictionary to check the spelling of the verbs.

Noun with -ion suffix	Base verb	Noun with -ion suffix	Base verb
collision		comprehension	
invasion		inclusion	
exclusion		confusion	
progression		confession	

3 Choose two of the words with suffixes from the table in the last activity. Write a creative sentence using both of them.

_____

_____

_____

_____

Now try this unit's 'Bringing it together' activity, which your teacher will give you.

Phonology

1 Think of some words you know from a subject you're learning about at the moment, such as geography, mathematics, or health and physical education. Find words from this topic to complete the table.

A word ...	
with two syllables	
with four syllables	
with an unaccented final syllable	
with an accented final syllable	
with four phonemes	
with six phonemes	
with a schwa in the final syllable	
with an **/ow/** diphthong	
with a **long /o/** phoneme	
ending with a vowel phoneme	
ending with a consonant digraph	
ending with a consonant blend	
with a vowel digraph	
with a medial short vowel phoneme	
with a **/f/** phoneme (unvoiced)	
with an unvoiced **/th/** phoneme	

Tip

A medial consonant doublet is a doubled consonant letter in the middle of a word. If the first syllable of a disyllabic word has a short vowel graph followed by one consonant, it is common for the consonant to be doubled. This is called a medial consonant doublet. 'Shallow' and 'simmer' have medial consonant doublets.

1 Write the missing consonant letter in each disyllabic word. Say each word and clap each syllable. Underline the letter that represents the short vowel in the first syllable of each word. The first word has been done for you. Use a dictionary to check your spelling.

muddle   tor_____ent   cur_____ent   nar_____ow

mel_____ow   shuf_____le   car_____y   baf_____le

stam_____er   hob_____le   but_____er   suf_____ix

gram_____ar   gal_____on   bat_____er   bit_____er

2 Sort these disyllabic words using the table.

| dimple | suffix | label | sample | stammer | silent |

| conflict | bitter | bellow | angle | compete | carry |

| hobble | socket | narrow | torrent |

Medial consonant is doubled   Medial consonant is not doubled

Circle the correctly spelled word in each pair. You may then use a dictionary to check your answers.

giggle	gigle	oppen	open
midle	middle	gurrgle	gurgle
window	winndow	craddle	cradle
chalenge	challenge	donate	donnate

1 Complete these activities by writing the base verb for each noun with a suffix. Use the rules about the suffix **-ion** as a guide. You may then use a dictionary to check the spelling of the verbs. The first word is done for you.

> **If the base verb ends in d, de or se, replace these letters with s and then add the suffix -ion.**

erosion: _____erode_____ extension: _____ fusion: _____

> **If the base verb ends in a vowel followed by t, replace the t with ss and then add the suffix -ion.**

permission: _____ admission: _____ emission: _____

> **If the base verb ends in a consonant followed by t, just add the suffix -ion.**

correction: _____ construction: _____ collection: _____

If the base **verb** ends in *te*, drop the *e* and then add the suffix *-ion*.

migration: _____ accommodation: _____ pollution: _____

If the base **verb** ends in *be*, replace *be* with *pt* and then add the suffix *-ion*.

description: _____ prescription: _____ transcription: _____

If the base **verb** ends in *ce*, replace the *e* with *t* and then add the suffix *-ion*.

introduction: _____ reduction: _____ production: _____

If the base **verb** ends in *ss*, just add the suffix *-ion*.

discussion: _____ progression: _____ confession: _____

Now try this unit's 'Bringing it together' activity, which your teacher will give you.

OS

X

Phonology

1 Think of some words you know from a subject you're learning about at the moment, such as geography, mathematics, or health and physical education. Find words from this topic to complete the table.

Two three-syllable words	
A four-syllable word	
A two-syllable word with an unaccented final syllable	
A two-syllable word with an accented final syllable	
A word with six phonemes	
A word with ten phonemes	
A word with a schwa in the final syllable	
A word with an **/oi/** diphthong	
A word with a **long /o/** phoneme	
A word with a medial short vowel phoneme	
A word ending with a vowel phoneme	
A word starting with a consonant digraph	
A word ending with a consonant digraph	
A word starting with a consonant blend	
A word ending with a consonant blend	
A word with a vowel digraph	

1 Scan a book you are reading to find words with the diphthong **/oi/**, as in 'toy' and 'coin'. You can also think of some other words you already know that have this sound. Then complete the table.

Base words that end with **oy**	
Words with **oy** in the initial accented syllable	
Base words that end with **oin**	
Base words that end with **oice**	
Base words that end with **oil**	
Base words that end with **oid**	
Other words with the **/oi/** diphthong	

2 Write the missing digraph in each word. Use **oy** or **oi** to complete the words. You may use a dictionary to check your spelling.

r_____al   aster_____d   ann_____ing   av_____d

conv_____s   destr_____ed   b_____sterous   ch_____ce

_____ster   disapp_____nt   v_____age   m_____st

OXFORD UNIVERSITY PRESS

1 Choose a base verb that fits each rule about the suffix *-ion*. Then use each rule to make a noun from the base verb. Finally, use each noun in a sentence.

> **If the base verb ends in *d*, *de* or *se*, replace these letters with *s* and then add the suffix *-ion*.**

Base verb: _____   Noun with **-ion** suffix: _____

Sentence: _____

_____

> **If the base verb ends in a consonant followed by *t*, just add the suffix *-ion*.**

Base verb: _____   Noun with **-ion** suffix: _____

Sentence: _____

_____

> **If the base verb ends in a vowel followed by *t*, replace the *t* with *ss* and then add the suffix *-ion*.**

Base verb: _____   Noun with **-ion** suffix: _____

Sentence: _____

_____

> **If the base verb ends in *te*, drop the *e* and then add the suffix *-ion*.**

Base verb: _____   Noun with **-ion** suffix: _____

Sentence: _____

_____

If the base verb ends in *be*, replace *be* with *pt* and then add the suffix *-ion*.

Base verb: _____   Noun with **-ion** suffix: _____

Sentence: _____

_____

If the base verb ends in *ce*, replace the *e* with *t* and then add the suffix *-ion*.

Base verb: _____   Noun with **-ion** suffix: _____

Sentence: _____

_____

If the base verb ends in *ss*, just add the suffix *-ion*.

Base verb: _____   Noun with **-ion** suffix: _____

Sentence: _____

_____

Now try this unit's 'Bringing it together' activity, which your teacher will give you.

1 Think of some words you know from a subject you're learning about at the moment, such as geography, mathematics, or health and physical education. Find words from this topic to complete the table.

A word with more than four syllables	
A word with four phonemes	
A word with more than 10 phonemes	
A word with a schwa in the final syllable	
A word with an **/ow/** diphthong	
A word with a **long /o/** phoneme	
A word that ends with a vowel phoneme	
A word that starts with a consonant digraph	
A word that ends with a consonant digraph	
A word that starts with a consonant blend	
A word that ends with a consonant blend	
A word with a vowel digraph	
A two-syllable word with an unaccented final syllable	
A two-syllable word with an accented final syllable	
A word with a medial short vowel phoneme	
A word with a **/f/** phoneme (unvoiced)	
A word with an unvoiced **/th/** phoneme	

OXFORD UNIVERSITY PRESS

1. These words have the diphthong **/ow/** (as in 'cow' and 'shout'). The digraph used to represent this phoneme is missing. Use either **ow** or **ou** to complete the words. You may then use a dictionary to check the spelling of each word.

p_____er   b_____nd   t_____el   g_____n   param_____nt

h_____se   gr_____l   dism_____nt   ab_____t   b_____el

s_____nd   acc_____nt   fr_____n   all_____   sp_____t

disc_____nt   t_____er   sh_____er   m_____se   v_____el

c_____ch   surr_____nd   cl_____n   v_____

2. Sort the words from the last activity using the table.

Words with **ow**	Words with **ou**

3 When are you likely to use the digraph **ow** to spell the diphthong **/ow/**? When are you more likely to use the digraph **ou** instead? Use the sentence starters to help you write your ideas.

I can use **ow** when …

I can use **ou** when …

The suffix **-ation** can change verbs to nouns.

Tip

1 Use these rules about the suffix **-ation** to complete the table on the next page. Two words are done for you.

If the base verb ends in y, it is common to replace the y with ic and then add the suffix -ation.

If the base verb ends in re, ve or se, it is common to remove the e and then add the suffix -ation.

OXFORD UNIVERSITY PRESS

Base verb	Noun ending in *-ation*
organise	organisation
magnify	magnification
inspire	
improvise	
prepare	
admire	
classify	
conserve	
realise	
observe	
identify	
converse	

2 Choose two of the words from the table in the last activity. Use the words in a creative sentence.

_____

_____

_____

Now try this unit's 'Bringing it together' activity, which your teacher will give you.

1 Think of some words you know from a subject you're learning about at the moment, such as geography, mathematics, or health and physical education. Find words from this topic to complete the table.

Two one-syllable words	
Two two-syllable words	
Two three-syllable words	
Two four-syllable words	
Two words with five phonemes	
Two words with six phonemes	
Two words with seven phonemes	
Two words with eight phonemes	

A word ...	
with a schwa in the final syllable	
with an **/ow/** diphthong	
with a **long /o/** phoneme	
ending with a vowel phoneme	
with a vowel digraph	
with a medial short vowel phoneme	
with a **/f/** phoneme (unvoiced)	

OXFORD UNIVERSITY PRESS

A word …	
with a **/v/** phoneme (voiced)	
with an unaccented final syllable	
with an accented final syllable	

1 Write these words in alphabetical order. Then write a sentence using each word. You may use a dictionary to help you.

frivolous   buffalo   affection

trough   sophisticated   affiliation

Word	Sentence

2 There are many ways to spell the **/f/** phoneme (as in 'fish'), which is unvoiced. Find the letter patterns that spell the **/f/** phoneme in the words. Sort the words using the table.

rough	paragraph	affiliation	fundraiser	confident	coughing	belief

phonological	effect	affection	biography	frivolous	sophisticated

toughest	buffalo	waffle	certificate	geography	trough	laughing

f	
ff	
ph	
gh	

Tip

A prefix is a group of letters that goes at the beginning of a word to make a new word.

Morphology

1 Use the chart to create words that start with the prefix **micro-**. Also add a suffix to each word. You may use a dictionary to help you. Write each word in the space on the next page.

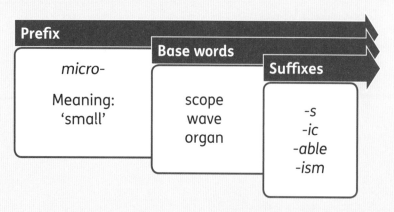

Prefix	Base words	Suffixes
micro- Meaning: 'small'	scope wave organ	-s -ic -able -ism

OXFORD UNIVERSITY PRESS

Words with the prefix *micro-*

---

2 Use the chart to create words that start with the prefix **semi-**. Also add a suffix to each word. You may use a dictionary to help you. Write each word in the space below.

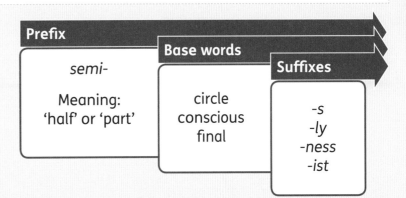

Prefix

semi-

Meaning: 'half' or 'part'

Base words

circle
conscious
final

Suffixes

-s
-ly
-ness
-ist

Words with the prefix *semi-*

---

3 Use the chart to create words that start with the prefix **multi-**. Also add a suffix to each word. You may use a dictionary to help you. Write each word in the space below.

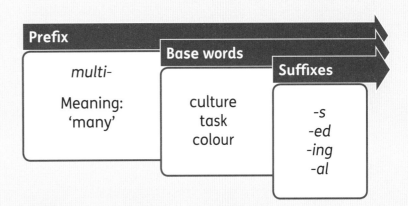

Prefix

multi-

Meaning: 'many'

Base words

culture
task
colour

Suffixes

-s
-ed
-ing
-al

Words with the prefix *multi-*

Now try this unit's 'Bringing it together' activity, which your teacher will give you.

1 Think of some words you know from a subject you're learning about at the moment, such as geography, mathematics, or health and physical education. Find words from this topic to complete the table.

Three one-syllable words	
A word with six syllables	
A word that has the same phoneme twice	
Three words with eight phonemes	
A word that starts with a schwa	
A word with an **/ow/** diphthong	
A word with a **long /o/** phoneme	
A word that ends with a vowel phoneme	
A word that starts with a consonant digraph	
A word that ends with a consonant digraph	
A word that starts with a consonant blend	
A word that ends with a consonant blend	
A word with a vowel digraph	

A two-syllable word with an unaccented final syllable	
A two-syllable word with an accented final syllable	
A word with a medial short vowel phoneme	
A word with a **/g/** phoneme	
A word with a **/j/** phoneme	

1 Write these words in alphabetical order. Then write a sentence using each word. You may use a dictionary to help you.

prologue   dialogue   epilogue   pigment

aghast   colleague

Word	Sentence

2 There are many ways to spell the **/g/** phoneme (as in 'egg'). Find the letter patterns that spell the **/g/** phoneme in the words. Sort the words using the chart.

choreography   dialogue   eggplant   yoghurt   aghast   dagger

investigate   plague   colleague   luggage   pigment   juggle

significant   ghetto   government   Afghanistan

prologue   smuggle   epilogue

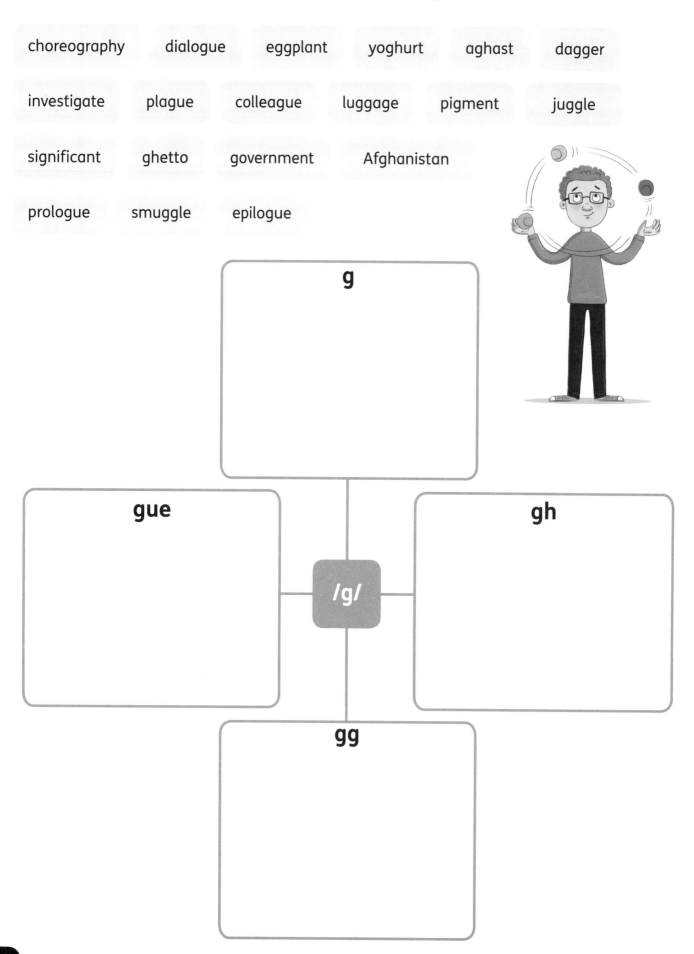

g

gue

gh

/g/

gg

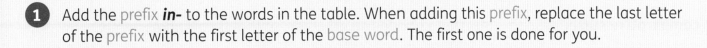

The prefix **in-** means 'not', 'the opposite' or 'without'.
It is common to absorb (or assimilate) **in-** into a base word that starts
with **l, m,** or **r.** In these words, the last letter of the prefix (**n**) is replaced
with the first letter of the base word.
For example, the prefix **in-** can be absorbed into the base word 'moderate' to
make a new word, 'immoderate', which means not moderate. 'Moderate' starts
with **m**, so the **n** in the prefix is replaced with another **m** to form 'immoderate'.

Tip

1. Add the prefix **in-** to the words in the table. When adding this prefix, replace the last letter
of the prefix with the first letter of the base word. The first one is done for you.

Prefix **in-** with last letter replaced	Base word	Word with prefix	Meaning of word with prefix
in ⟶ il	legal	illegal	Not legal
	logical		
	literate		
	mobile		
	mature		
	moral		
	rational		
	responsible		
	relevant		
	regular		

Now try this unit's 'Bringing
it together' activity, which your
teacher will give you.

GLOSSARY

accented syllable	the syllable in a word that has the strongest emphasis *the first syllable in 'apple' and the second syllable in 'believe'*
adjective	a word that tells us what something is like *small, tall, funny*
base word	the smallest part of a word that is also a word on its own *the word 'jump' in 'jumping'*
blend	speech sounds that join together in a word ***/st/** is a blend in the word 'stop'*
comparative suffix	a suffix that changes an adjective so that it compares nouns ***-er** in 'shorter', 'bigger', 'louder'*
compound word	a new word made out of two words joined together *sunshine (sun + shine), playground (play + ground)*
consonant	a speech sound made by blocking some air with your lips, teeth or tongue ***/b/**, **/l/**, **/z/**, **/v/***
consonant digraph	two letters representing one consonant sound ***sh**, **ch**, **th***
digraph	two letters representing one phoneme ***sh**, **ch**, **oo**, **ee**, **ie***
diphthong	a kind of long vowel sound that you make by moving your mouth in two ways ***/oi/** in 'boy', **/ow/** in 'cow'*
disyllabic word	a word with two syllables *monster (mon-ster), sunshine (sun-shine)*
etymology	the study of where words come from and how they change over time *the word 'pizza' comes from a Latin word and an Italian dialect word meaning 'to clamp' or 'to stamp'*
graph	one letter representing one phoneme ***b**, **w**, **o***
homophone	a word that sounds the same as another word but looks different and has a different meaning *eight, ate*
medial consonant doublet	a doubled consonant letter in the middle of a word ***bb** in 'bubble'*
medial	in the middle. A medial phoneme is a speech sound in the middle of a word. This can be a medial vowel or a medial consonant. ***/o/** is the medial phoneme in the word 'dog'*
morpheme	the smallest unit of meaning in a word *'jumped' has two parts with meaning (**jump** and **-ed**)*
noun	a word that is a name for something, such as a person, place, animal, thing or idea *Ali, school, cat, ball, age, protection*

OXFORD UNIVERSITY PRESS

onset	the sounds in a syllable before the vowel *b represents the onset in the word 'big'*
phoneme	the smallest speech sound you can hear in a word *the word 'boot' has three phonemes:* **/b/**, **long /oo/** *and* **/t/**
plural	a word for more than one thing *'hats' is the plural of the word 'hat'*
prefix	letters that go at the beginning of a word to make a new word **un-** *in 'unhappy' means 'not' (un- + happy = not happy)*
regular verb	a verb that takes the suffix **-ed** to make the past tense *'jump' + -ed = jumped*
rime	the vowel and other speech sounds at the end of a syllable **ig** *represents the rime in the word 'big'*
r-influenced vowel	a vowel that sounds different because it is followed by the letter **r** **/er/** *in 'mermaid',* **/air/** *in 'chair'*
schwa	an **/uh/** sound in a word *the* **a** *in 'balloon' sounds like* **/uh/**
suffix	letters that go at the end of a word to make a new word *the* **-s** *in 'cats' means 'more than one cat'*
superlative suffix	a suffix that means 'most' **-est** *in 'biggest', 'smallest'*
syllable	a part of a word that feels like a beat and has a vowel sound *'weekend' has two syllables (week-end)*
tense	the way a word is written that shows whether something is in the past, present or future *'jumped' means the jumping happened in the past*
trigraph	three letters representing one phoneme **igh** *in 'might'*
unvoiced phoneme	a sound made using your breath rather than your voice **/th/** *in 'bath'*
verb	a word for something that happens *'play' is the verb in the sentence 'I play chess.'*
voiced phoneme	a sound made using your voice **/th/** *in 'the'*
vowel	a sound that you voice with your mouth open and not blocked by your lips, teeth or tongue *the* **short /o/** *sound in the word 'dog' is a vowel sound*

When you have finished the activities in each unit, think about how you feel about the work you have completed.

Draw a ✓ if you feel confident using these ideas on your own.

Draw a ✗ if you feel you need to learn more.

Draw a ○ if you are not sure.

Unit	Phonology	Orthography	Morphology
1			
2			
3			
4			
5			
6			
7			
8			
9			
10			
11			
12			
13			
14			
15			
16			
17			
18			
19			
20			
21			
22			
23			
24			
25			
26			
27			
28			

OXFORD UNIVERSITY PRESS